Mother Day - 2002
From Treasa + Terry

D15Ø6458

To:

_____

From:

_____

I remember your hands...

_____

_____

_____

_____

_____

Thank you for touching my life with such love.

My Mother's Hands

CELEBRATING HER SPECIAL TOUCH

JOHN TRENT, PH.D. *with* ERIN M. HEALY

WATERBROOK
PRESS

MY MOTHER'S HANDS
PUBLISHED BY WATERBROOK PRESS
5446 North Academy Boulevard, Suite 200
Colorado Springs, Colorado 80918
A division of Random House, Inc.

The original stories that open each chapter of this book are fictional. Although they are
loosely based on real events, they do not represent any specific person or occasion.

All scripture quotations, unless otherwise indicated, are taken from the *Holy Bible,
New International Version*®. NIV®. Copyright © 1973, 1978, 1984 by International
Bible Society. Used by permission of Zondervan Publishing House. All rights reserved.
Scripture quotations marked (KJV) are taken from the King James Version of the Bible.

ISBN 1-57856-327-5

These publishers have generously given permission to used extended quotations
from the following copyrighted works: From *The Web of Life* by Richard Louv,
© 1997 by Richard Louv, by permission of Conari Press. From *Mothers & Daughters*
by Madeleine L'Engle, © 1997 by Crosswicks. Used by permission of Harold Shaw
Publishers, Wheaton, IL 60189. From *Mothering by Heart,* © 1996, by Robin Jones
Gunn. Used by permission of Multnomah Publishers, Inc. From *Praying the Bible
for Your Children* by David and Heather Kopp, © 1997 by David and Heather Kopp.
Used by permission of WaterBrook Press. From *HeartPrints* by Sandra P. Aldrich
and Bobbie Valentine, © 1998 by Sandra Picklesimer Aldrich and Bobbie Valentine.
Used by permission of WaterBrook Press.

Printed in the United States of America

2000—First Edition

10 9 8 7 6 5 4 3 2

My life has been graced by watching two mothers' hands at work.
One, my own precious mother,
who loved and blessed her three sons.
The other, my priceless wife, Cindy.
Her hands have helped shape our two daughters
into wonderful young women, full of love for their Savior.
I am doubly blessed and dedicate this book to each of you.
—J.T.

To Boo's Mom,
whose hands make an appearance in many of these stories.
—E.H.

Table of Contents

FASCINATION

Mother let me play with one of her hands. She laid it flat on a living-room end table beside her chair. I picked up a transverse pinch of skin over the knuckle of her index finger and let it drop. The pinch didn't snap back; it lay dead across her knuckle in a yellowish ridge. I poked it; it slid over intact. I left it there as an experiment and shifted to another finger. Mother was reading *Time* magazine.

Carefully, lifting it by the tip, I raised her middle finger an inch and released it. It snapped back to the tabletop. Her insides, at least, were alive. I tried all the fingers. They all worked. Some I could lift higher than others.

"That's getting boring."

"Sorry, Mama."

I refashioned the ridge on her index-finger knuckle; I made the ridge as long as I could, using both my hands. Moving quickly, I made parallel ridges on her other fingers—a real mountain chain, the Alleghenies; Indians crept along just below the ridge-tops, eyeing the frozen lakes below them through the trees.

—ANNIE DILLARD, *An American Childhood*

Hands That Bless

Because my twin brother and I were only two months old when our father left, I didn't hear the shock in my mother's voice when she picked up the phone and he told her he was moving out. I didn't hear her cry. I didn't understand the despair she felt as a suddenly single parent with no job, no college degree, no money, no help from her family or the government.

In 1952 the divorce rate was four couples per thousand. No, that's not a typo. Per thousand. Suddenly she was not only in a minority but a minority that was looked down upon by the vast majority of society. She went to business school and became a career woman in the early '50s, a pioneer by circumstances, not by choice. She was the thirteenth employee at First Federal Savings and Loan and ascended to the level of first-vice-president. Because of her accomplishment of opening thirteen branches in 1956, the *Wall Street Journal* did a story on her.

But despite her accomplishments, her career was always secondary to her three sons, Joe, Jeff, and John.

Although she was solely responsible for supporting my brothers and me, she also got us involved in sports, took us camping, put posters of sports heroes up on our walls, and took us to see the Dodgers when they came to Phoenix for spring training, giving us a chance to see in real life some of the heroes in our lives such as Sandy Koufax and Don Drysdale.

She was an incredible woman.

When I think of my childhood, my thoughts range over a thousand pictures of my mother's hands. By the time I was ten, my mother's hands were bent and twisted with rheumatoid arthritis. The world wouldn't think them beautiful, but they were beautiful to me and to my brothers. They became, over the years, a symbol of her love for us.

Because of the pain in those twisted joints, my mother could not grab your hand. She never took your hand and shook it. When she took it, she touched it gently, squeezing just a part of it. Holding on to you softly. Then releasing you from her touch.

That's how she held on to each of us boys. Tenderly. Softly. With great affection and warmth.

Yet loosely. The day Jeff and I turned sixteen she took us to get our driver's licenses. Thirty minutes later she let us drive our old Volkswagen twelve hundred miles from Phoenix to Indianapolis to see our uncle. She wanted to go with us, but her hands and knees were too pained to sit scrunched in a small car for that long. Every time I look back, I marvel at the loose hold she had on our lives.

She held everything loosely. Cups. Silverware. Pencils. She even held the days loosely, never knowing whether it would be a good day or a bad one, taking what came and taking it with grace. If her gentle touch helped us to grow up, it also provided a strong incentive to do what was right. Because her hands hurt so much, my mother was never able to spank us, but beneath her tender ways there lay an underlying firmness. Worse than a spanking was her way of placing her hand on ours, always softly, and speaking to us, always gently, of her concern about our behavior. When she looked up at you and held your hand, you might as well have been in the grip of a lumberjack. You couldn't pull away. It would hurt her hands if you did. So you sat there. And you listened. And little by little, the warmth of her heart melted yours.

Whatever I lost in a dad, I gained in a mom. She was the compensating grace in my life. She was like Job in many ways. She hadn't deserved the divorce or the disease. Yet she refused to complain, much less to curse God. In spite of the pain, she carried on with love, with purpose, with dignity. She never gave up, never turned despondent.

Her hands couldn't iron my slacks or sew buttons on my shirts or tie my ties. She couldn't do much with her hands. Yet with them she taught me everything—a picture at a time, a blessing at a time.

What pictures of your mother's hands do you carry in your memory?

Perhaps you see them folding a damp washcloth and laying it gently on your fevered forehead or clapping for you when you scored that goal. Perhaps you see her hands typing that term paper late at night, or waving to you at graduation, or praying for you during that time of your deepest hurt.

That's what this book is all about.

Snapshots, Polaroids, pictures of the many ways in which a mother's hands provide and create and comfort and teach and discipline and protect and pray.

Did you know that Michelangelo believed that the hardest feature to capture in his sculptures were his subjects' *hands?* That's because they were so unique and because they carried so much of a person's character.

If your mother is living, these reflections can give you a wonderful way of saying to her, "Thank you," or "I love you," or "You never gave up on me." If you've lost your mother, as I have, I pray that these pictures will give you yet another reason for thanking the Lord for the mom He gave you—something precious to hold on to between here and heaven.

May each reflection, each thought, each picture that follows bring back loving memories as we celebrate our mothers' hands.

—John Trent
President, Encouraging Words
www.strongfamilies.com

Yours were the first fingers to find mine

The first hands to hold mine

The first touches that would guide me for a lifetime

ONE

Hands That Create

A mother's eternal fingerprints

Every mother is like Moses. She does not
enter the promised land. She prepares a world
she will never see.

—POPE PAUL VI

It took a little doing to reach the workbench in the garage where Mom was assembling a bouquet of Casablanca lilies. A pile of laundry pointed the way. Laundry, everywhere. And poinsettias. Two dozen, to be exact, in full Christmas bloom. And silver baskets. And floral foam. And five-gallon buckets full of red and white roses. A bolt of silver ribbon had tangled itself in a mess of floral wires and vases.

Chaos. Terrific chaos. I navigated the flower-strewn concrete toward a stool.

It was late and chilly. The scents of December and refrigerated flowers mingled with cinnamon and hot apple cider. A most wondrous smell. Mom held up five red roses next to the white bouquet. "What do you think?"

I hesitated. "Don't go overboard on the red."

"I won't. But it needs a little."

I trusted her judgment on this. I usually did, although I was getting better at trusting my own gut, too. I rested my elbows on the table and watched her work. She was right about the red. *How does she do that?* Soft Christmas music came from the windowsill. I glanced at our little portable radio. Trusty as ever.

My mind drifted. Twenty years ago, I had rested my elbows on a similar table. Mom was drawing something for her class at the university. I sat next to her in awe. The table was huge. The classroom was huge. The charcoal figures she bent over were huge. *How does she do that?*

I spent a great deal of my childhood asking that question, full of awe. Good night, Martha Stewart—you couldn't hold a candle to my mom. She knew how to make a home. My dad and siblings and I knew how to live in it. We reveled in its comfort. In her special touches. A chest of drawers bearing hand-drawn scenes from *Alice in Wonderland*. The special paper and paint in each one's bedroom. Hot candle wax shaped into something medieval before it cooled. Household plants dangling in macramé hangers. Handel's *Messiah*, blasting us out of bed at dawn. A shadow box full of mementos from my father's Air Force career. Homemade applesauce. Decorative windows frosted with a sandblaster. Sand, tracked into the house for weeks. Sand. Everywhere, sand.

How did she do that?

Memories of home went with me to college. They stayed with me afterward. Of course they would. I weighed the aesthetics of creating a similar home against the financial cost of doing so. I was too frugal. I eschewed the extras of life. Splurging, I called it. Couldn't afford that. Not on my meager postgraduate salary. I settled for beach towels instead of curtains. Kept the bedspread I'd had since high school. Tried not to notice my blank white walls.

There is nothing wrong with simplicity (you could call it that, I suppose). But I soon missed those touches of my mother's. Touches that made a house a home. We talked about it one day when she came to visit. She had brought me a wreath for my front door. Sweet-smelling eucalyptus. I was surprised by how much I liked it.

"Give yourself permission to see that aesthetic things are important to you," she had said. The thought stopped me for a moment. *How does she do that?*

I loosened up a bit. I bought the scented candle here, the cheery flowers there. They added a lot to my own home. But not everything. I soon realized how insignificant *things* are. Their true significance lies in the memories they evoke—and create. My mother's eternal investment will never be found in material items, but in the warmth and caring they represent. Every gesture, every artistic decision, every idea that ever took seed in her mind, all speak of her desire to create a comfortable haven for her family. Even the clutter—terrific chaos!—of the creative process testifies to her love for us.

The bouquet—white with just the right amount of red—was finished. Beautiful. She picked her way around the table and held it low at my hips. "Carry it here," she instructed. "Not too high, or you'll look nervous."

"I am nervous," I laughed.

"You're gorgeous," she said. "The most confident bride ever. Tomorrow will be a special day."

"These flowers will make it all the more special," I told her.

"Anything for you, hon." She gave me a kiss on the forehead. She'd be up for a while, putting finishing touches on other arrangements. "See you bright and early."

I made my way back through the cider scent and crawled into bed for one last night in my childhood home. Ah. Fuzzy flannel sheets. Soon I would make a home for my husband. Maybe someday children. I fell asleep thinking of creating a similar place, full of similar memories, for them. *How would I do that?*

The Art Chest

It was a small piece of furniture, perhaps an old washstand, with three drawers.... This chest had held my mother's art supplies. She made her living as a greeting card artist. She began working in Kansas City, at age sixteen, for Hallmark Cards, and over the years became known as one of the best freelance greeting card artists.

I grew up watching her work. I would stand next to her art table and watch her hand move the brush expertly across the paper and then move to the right, to the chest, where she would dip it into blotches of paint or stir the brush loudly in an old fruit jar of water.

The paints and an airbrush and her heavy tape dispenser and her scissors were kept there. From time to time, the tape or the scissors would disappear, and she would call out irritated to her two boys to bring them back. But she never banned us from her desk. The squares of blotter paper she cut out were just right for our drawings, and our drawings littered the floor below the table.

Over the years, she covered the chest with layers of spilled paint and ink and tattooed it with cigarette burns. She was always leaving her cigarettes burning.

A couple of weekends ago, I decided that the time had come to go through the chest and refinish it and give it a new life.... I spent the next six hours bent over the chest, leaning into the grain.

Perhaps it was the noise from the electric sander, or the repetitive motion, or the concentration, but as I wore away the years, I heard my mother's voice. We talked all afternoon.

"Richy, your drawing is wonderful." A deep red stain was fading. "Have you seen my tape?" I heard her laughing.... "I don't like antiques. I like contemporary." She told me about my grandmother, and about my grandfather. The green lifted. "See what your brother's up to." Cigarette burns vanished. "Do it right or don't do it at all." I heard a sound like the ringing of a bell. It was my mother's brush in the old fruit jar.

Year after year, decade after decade, perhaps even a century, lifted from the wood.

The sawdust began to smell fresher, newer, expectant.

I stood back and looked at the chest. A few of my mother's marks remained. I thought: Perhaps I have gone too far; I should have left more of her there.

I heard her say she was pleased.

The chest, now quiet, is in our family room.

It remains unfinished.

—RICHARD LOUV, *The Web of Life*

Home Sweet Home

I gaze on the moon as I tread the drear wild,
And feel that my mother now thinks of her child,
As she looks on that moon from our own cottage door
Thro' the woodbine, whose fragrance shall cheer me no more.
  Home, home, sweet, sweet home!
There's no place like home, oh, there's no place like home!

—JOHN HOWARD PAYNE

Radio speaker, author, and mother Mary Whelchel is enchanted with eagles and with the spiritual lessons we can see in their nest-building practices. Listening to her describe the finishing touches on an eagle's nest, I was pierced by the mother eagle's investment in her home. It seems that once she builds the eight-foot by ten-foot monstrous nest (which has been said to look like a bonfire waiting for a match), she then softens the nest by plucking down from her own chest. Adding a fluffy bit here and there, like pillows accenting a color scheme in a living room, the mother eagle completes her nest with an offering of her own body.

—ELISA MORGAN, *Meditations for Mothers*

TWO

Hands That Provide

A mother's diligent work

If what has hitherto been woman's work in the world
is simply left undone by them, there is no one else
to take it up. If…their old and special work is neglected
and only half done, there will be something seriously
wrong with the world, for the commonplace home
work of women is the very foundation
upon which everything else rests.

—LAURA INGALLS WILDER

GWYNNETH'S STORY

Mother adjusted the spectacles in front of her dim vision with an unsteady hand and then returned it to her lap for the waiting. I was taking her over to the hotel to see the fresh flowers, I had explained, just a fifty-yard stroll from her front door.

"Darlene has arranged them herself," I told her. Darlene was my second child. "You'll surely want to see them, Mother. It's the first fresh batch this spring. Besides, you know how much everyone loves you to drop by."

"Heaven knows why," she had murmured. "I'm afraid I don't keep up my acquaintances very well these days." I scolded her nonsense by raising an eyebrow. I finished teasing her hair and then helped her don her beaded fuchsia sweater, a favorite that made her eyes equally bright. Her hands were too frail to do the buttons anymore, although she tried. She was still proud and stubborn even now, at one hundred years old.

Her wheelchair rattled as I pushed it down the lane toward the lobby. "The roses are beautiful," she said, breaking the silence. "Manuel has done good work. Tell him I said so."

"I will, Mother." A compliment from Mother always went a long way with those who knew her excruciating perfectionism. Decades earlier, her frequent visits to the hotel were cause for some panic among her employees. They simultaneously loved and feared her, this woman who could spot a wrinkled bedspread while she was still in the hallway, who could tell with a mere sniff whether Chef had used enough milk in the Irish oatmeal. Nevertheless, this five-foot-two fury worked as hard as she expected everyone else to and so endeared herself to everyone she ever hired.

Apart from her indomitable nature I don't think the hotel would have made it. She and Father bought the place when I was only two, seventy-five years ago, and the quaint lakeside inn became as much home to me as any house might have been. Back then, as the Roaring Twenties waned, so had the hotel. Rundown and overgrown by the time my parents relieved the previous owners of it, the deteriorated property provided Mother and Father with both an investment opportunity and an irresistible challenge.

Every afternoon my brothers and I hastened home from school and did our chores with reckless speed. "I expect you home in time for supper!" Mother always yelled after us as we then bolted for the lake. While we splashed each other to soaking and hunted the reeds for frogs, Mother worked—and she continued into the night, breaking only to make us supper and track us down to come eat it. Then she picked up her work again, mending Father's good trousers while helping us with our homework, or taking tea to late-arrived guests, or cleaning up the restaurant kitchen after washing all the dishes in our own. I never saw Mother not working. Or not happy.

A good bit of the happiness disappeared one night twelve years later. A rainy night, a slick road, a drunken sailor on weekend leave....

Father went out to call on Grandmama and never returned, his motorcar struck on a curve by the sailor's own careening truck.

Mother cried inconsolably and without apology when Uncle Joe arrived with the news. My mother, the stoic woman never before shaken by any event, was momentarily devastated. She mourned the loss of her helpmate, the father of her children, her lover. Although she never spoke of it to us, I would think she silently considered giving it all up. A single mother with a business to run and global war looming large on the horizon.... The odds frowned at her.

Within weeks of Father's death, however, Mom found solace in her work and her family. My oldest brother was preparing for college. She insisted that he go. She would double her efforts, save for his schooling, and expect the rest of us to follow suit.

The hotel needed repair. She set pride aside and asked family members to do what Father would have done himself. A local overburdened seamstress gave Mother extra tasks so she could pay the bills that the hotel could not cover during the slow winter months. She waited tables and cleaned rooms and kept fresh flowers in the lobby. Always, always, fresh flowers adorned the lobby.

"This place is your inheritance," she would say at the end of the day, soaking her feet and nursing her cracked hands. "I plan to leave it to you in pristine condition."

By the time my brother returned from the war, "pristine" was exactly the word to describe Mother's piece of earth. Visitors flocked to celebrate with loved ones the end of troubling times. Most folks in our little town knew Mother by name, and they often dropped in for luncheon just to check on her. The mayor granted our little inn land-mark status.

The years went by and the business grew. So did our family, and the inheritance Mother planned to leave us became our place of gathering. Her sprawling ranch-style home, nestled in a private spot on the hotel property, bustled with grandchildren and great-grandchildren. We held weddings in her garden, Christmas in her front room, and lakeside parties on any occasion that suited us. Over time her smiles came ever more readily, even as her body and ability to work slowed.

Today a simple trip to the lobby is an all-day affair that exhausts her more than a full day as a single mother ever did. But on occasion I can talk her into going to see Manuel's fresh flowers, to sit by the fireplace, to take tea with a few regulars who haven't yet forgotten her name.

I pushed the rattling wheelchair onto the quiet hotel patio and paused underneath the blooming wisteria.

"Surprise!"

Her youngest great-grandchildren were first to burst through the double doors and rush at her with kisses and hugs—a herd of elephants, surely. "Happy birthday!" the four-year-old squealed, even though it wasn't quite. But that was what we had gathered to cele-brate, all five hundred friends and family members who came tum-bling out after the children.

"Oh my," was all Mother was able to muster in her surprise as she placed her gnarled, beautiful hands to her chest. Big-band sounds began to rise from the gardens, and I slowly pushed her chair in that direction as the gurgling mob swirled around her. She began to laugh, and a smile wider than her broad spectacles made her eyes sparkle.

She grabbed my hand and held it tightly. "I cannot believe so many people would come," she whispered loudly in my ear. I squeezed gently. I myself was not surprised at all.

A mother lays down her life for her child and for her home, but there is nothing advertised in her doing it. If the mother were to tell her child what she was doing, it would be an abortion of motherhood. The child will never recognize what the mother has done until in years to come the child is in the same place. Only then will the unadvertised substitution of the mother's life and love be recognized.

—OSWALD CHAMBERS, *The Love of God*

She sets about her work vigorously;
*   her arms are strong for her tasks.*
She sees that her trading is profitable,
*   and her lamp does not go out at night.*
In her hand she holds the distaff
*   and grasps the spindle with her fingers....*

She watches over the affairs of her household
and does not eat the bread of idleness.
Her children arise and call her blessed;
her husband also, and he praises her.

—PROVERBS 31:17-19,27-28

In all the little daily patterns of the home—the laundry going into the same hamper, the sweaters into the same drawer, the hair getting washed and the shoes polished on Saturday nights—God is at work. He delights to glorify Himself in the commonplace.... He made our little daily chores channels of His grace.

—ANNE ORTLUND

"Templeton," said Wilbur, "if you weren't so dopey, you would have noticed that Charlotte has made an egg sac. She is going to become a mother. For your information, there are five hundred and fourteen eggs in that peachy little sac."

—E. B. WHITE, *Charlotte's Web*

THREE

Hands That Comfort

A mother's gentle touch

A mother is the truest friend we have, when trials
heavy and sudden fall upon us; when adversity takes
the place of prosperity; when friends who rejoice with
us in our sunshine desert us; when troubles thicken
around us; still will she cling to us, and endeavor by
her kind precepts and counsels to dissipate the clouds
of darkness, and cause peace to return to our hearts.

—WASHINGTON IRVING

NATHAN'S STORY

No way was I going to spend my twenty-first birthday laid flat-out on my back. Finals were over, and my rafting trip was on. No way in the world was I going to miss it.

"I'm goin' with you to the Rogue," I announced to my roommate Dave.

"Yeah, right." Dave shook his head. "Dude, you're a mess."

The doc looked grim. "You separated your shoulder and twisted your knee," he said with all the grimness of Spock. "You've torn things in there that shouldn't be torn. Surgery. Thursday. You won't be going anywhere for a while." He wrote a prescription for painkillers and left the room.

"Just sign my death warrant, why don't you," I muttered to his back.

Against my will, by Friday afternoon I found myself immobilized, flat on my back in my tiny apartment, watching daytime TV, popping painkillers, and thinking of Dave and the gang ripping down the river. Jimmy Stewart in *Rear Window* had it better than I did. Especially in not having to deal with boredom. The guys who hadn't gone to the river had gone home to visit their moms, with the coming Sunday being Mother's Day and all.

So there I lay, feeling sorry for myself and only a tad guilty that I wouldn't make it home to visit my own mom, who lived four hours away. She'd planned on my being at the river anyway, so I convinced myself it was no big deal. I called her during a commercial break to explain recent events. She didn't even think twice. "I'm coming up," she announced. "I'll be there tomorrow evening. We'll watch your favorite old movies or something." I hung up the phone a bit stunned but looking forward to her company.

Then it hit, on Saturday afternoon. None other than the flu. Doc said it was probably something I picked up at the hospital, of all places, where my injured and susceptible body couldn't fight it off. Go figure. By the time Mom arrived that night I was a wreck, a raging headache and fever preventing me from doing anything beyond making it to the bathroom. I didn't even hear Mom come in.

But then she was there, her hand gentle on my healthy shoulder. The relief of not having to be sick *and* alone gave me the strength to get back to the sofa.

"You used to beg me to let you stay in the living room when you were sick," she practically whispered, helping me along. "You hated being in your room. It made you feel too isolated." Somewhere in my fever that memory surfaced, and I managed a smile. She set up a coffee-table sick station.

"Oh, Mom—don't mess with that." My protest was feeble, and she ignored me.

She mopped my forehead and fed me chicken broth. I gave up and let her cover me with a blanket. I was five years old again and glad my roommates were gone. I drifted off to sleep.

Next thing I knew it was Monday. She looked up from the book she was reading in the chair next to me and smiled.

"You look better," she said.

"Right." My shoulder still throbbed. I shifted to get comfortable.

"Well, you do. Anyway, I'd hate that birthday cake I brought over to go to waste." She winked at me.

My birthday? *Mother's Day.* I'd completely missed it. I groaned. "Oh, Mom—I'm sorry. I don't even have a gift…"

"What do you mean? I brought you one." She pointed to a small package on the table.

"No. For you. Mother's Day. I missed it."

She waved her hand and shook her head. "You didn't miss a thing," she insisted. "I got to spend the weekend with my son. You're the best Mother's Day present I ever did get. Now open it."

Leave it to Mom to serve me on a day when the tables should have been turned. She would have done it any day, I know. Once a mom, always a mom, although I guess I'll never fully understand that. But I don't object.

I tore at the paper. *Casablanca.* One of the best movies ever made. "Dude!" I laughed. "This is great. But I already have a copy."

"No—you have *my* copy." She grinned. "And when I leave I'll be taking it back with me. So since I haven't been able to watch it for a while, what do you say we have Mother's Day this morning and watch it together?"

I agreed it would be a perfect way to spend the morning. She popped in the tape.

Ain't Afeared of Hummin' Birds

That night I couldn't sleep.

"What's wrong, child?" Moe Moe Bay said from her chair.

"I don't want to go back," I blurted out.

"I know, child," she said. "Of course you don't."

"You don't understand. I took up and run away from my unit. I was hit when I was runnin'." I sobbed so hard my ribs hurt. "I'm a coward and a deserter."

She looked at the fire and said nothing for the longest time. Then her voice covered my cries. "You ain't nothin' of the kind. You a child...a child! Of course you scared. Ain't nobody that ain't."

"I'm not brave like Pink.... I'm not brave."

"Child, bein' brave don't mean you ain't afeared. Don't you know that?"

"I don't want to die."

"They's things worse than death, child. But you got nothin' to fear. You are here now, and I'm huggin' you up. You goin' to be an old man someday. When it is your time, the sweet Lord'll send a hummin' bird to fly your soul to heaven. Now, you ain't afeared of hummin' birds, are you?"

Her words brought me sweet sleep. That night I dreamt of hummin' birds and green pastures full of sunlight and wildflowers.

—PATRICIA POLACCO, *Pink and Say*

Kiss

I said to my mother, "You don't understand. It was different when you were my age. Kids didn't think the way we do know. You don't get it."

I said to my friend, "You don't understand. How could you let me down this way? How could you do without me?"

I said to God, "You don't understand. You're mean."

I went to bed. I stuck my head under the covers and wouldn't say good night to anyone.

I woke up in the middle of the night. My covers had all been straightened out. My old bear had been put on the pillow beside me. Like a kiss. My mother's kiss.

God's kiss.

—MADELEINE L'ENGLE, *Mothers and Daughters*

Led by Mother's Hand

"I gave my best to the country I love, and kept my tears till he was gone. Why should I complain, when we both have merely done our duty and will surely be the happier for it in the end? If I don't seem to need help, it is because I have a better friend, even than father, to comfort and sustain me. My child, the troubles and temptations of your life are beginning, and may be many; but you can overcome and outlive them all if you learn to feel the strength and tenderness of your Heavenly Father as you do that of your earthly one. The more you love and trust Him, the nearer you will feel to Him, and the less you will depend on human power and wisdom. His love and care never tire or change, can never be taken from you, but may become the source of lifelong peace, happiness, and strength. Believe this heartily, and go to God with all your little cares, and hopes, and sins, and sorrows, as freely and confidingly as you come to your mother."

Jo's only answer was to hold her mother close, and, in the silence which followed, the sincerest prayer she had ever prayed left her heart without words; for in that sad, yet happy hour, she had learned not only the bitterness of remorse and despair, but the sweetness of self-denial and self-control; and, led by her mother's hand, she had drawn nearer to the Friend who welcomes every child with a love stronger than that of any father, tenderer than that of any mother.

—LOUISA MAY ALCOTT, *Little Women*

My Mother

Who fed me from her gentle breast
And hushed me in her arms to rest,
And on my cheek sweet kisses prest?
My mother.

When sleep forsook my open eye,
Who was it sung sweet lullaby
And rocked me that I should not cry?
My mother.

Who sat and watched my infant head
When sleeping in my cradle bed,
And tears of sweet affection shed?
    My mother.

When pain and sickness made me cry,
Who gazed upon my heavy eye
And wept, for fear that I should die?
    My mother.

Who ran to help me when I fell
And would some pretty story tell,
Or kiss the part to make it well?
    My mother.

Who taught my infant lips to pray,
To love God's holy word and day,
And walk in wisdom's pleasant way?
    My mother.

And can I ever cease to be
Affectionate and kind to thee
Who wast so very kind to me,—
    My mother.

Oh no, the thought I cannot bear;
And if God please my life to spare
I hope I shall reward thy care,
My mother.

When thou art feeble, old and gray,
My healthy arm shall be thy stay,
And I will soothe thy pains away,
My mother.

And when I see thee hang thy head,
'Twill be my turn to watch thy bed,
And tears of sweet affection shed,—
My mother.

—ANN TAYLOR

FOUR

Hands That Discipline

A mother's tough love

My mother had a great deal of trouble with me
but I think she enjoyed it.

—MARK TWAIN

I keep my dresses hung neatly on special tangle-proof hangers. In the closet. Where the cats (my perpetually shedding cats!) can't sit on them. Where my hubby's muddy shoes won't dirty them.

I wasn't always so tidy.

My darling mother is not a neat-nick—heavens no!—and I suppose I inherited my lack of this quality from her. But she was admirable in her refusal to believe she had to have certain qualities mastered before she could begin teaching them to her children. Not that being neat is the epitome of godly living (who would think it?), but it has its place.

Now they say good character is the outcome of consistently healthy childhood discipline. (I would agree.) They also say that all children need custom-tailored discipline in order for it to have any effect upon their lives. As far as my mother was concerned she could have opened up shop as a Discipline Seamstress. Without a doubt God knew that a child as creative as I would need a mother like her.

Take, for example, the time she managed to give me a straight-faced speech on the consequences of disrupting church—I was four—after she removed my fidgety body from the sanctuary while I screamed, "But Jesus lives in MY heart, so how can He live in YOURS?!" Then there was the time I sassed Father when I was eight (I'm ashamed of it to this day), and she decided I would remain home with a sitter while the entire family attended *my* school carnival *without me*. There was also the time she walked me to the bus stop—I was fourteen—dressed in hair curlers and Miss Piggy slippers because I'd mocked a schoolmate's unsophisticated parents behind their backs. I couldn't *believe* it.

And then there was The Dress Episode.

I was six going on sixteen. Sophisticated. Fashionable. My dresses were tantamount to my image. Before I would even consider wearing a particular dress, I required it to meet a single essential criterion: It must twirl. In other words, it must have just the right poof-factor— the skirt must rise high enough to touch my ballerina hands, yet stay low enough to keep my panties hidden at all times. I *loved* my dresses.

But, along with the rest of my things, I did not love putting them away where they belonged. (Is there a child who does?) After wearing them only once—never more!—I draped them over the back of my chair or kicked them under my bed, passing them over in favor of fresher, crisply ironed dresses until the following week's laundry.

Of course, Mother got tired of washing and pressing otherwise clean dresses and instructed me a dozen times to keep them (and my closet and my bedroom) in order. A dozen times she showed me how, and a dozen times I languished in the sterility of an immaculate room until the second law of thermodynamics took it over again. She finally issued an ultimatum. Clean up—or else!

Fine, I thought. I deposited everything I owned into my oak bench box (a truly beautiful piece of woodwork) and called it a day.

My dresses wouldn't fit inside, but I quickly realized it would take too much time and effort to untangle the hangers in my closet and put the dresses where they belonged. I was a busy young lady with more important things to do. So I dropped them behind the box and mashed it against the wall as far as I could.

Mother found them.

I was twirling down the hall after having had a sumptuous tea with my dolls when I discovered her in my room quietly cleaning out my closet. Every dress I owned was on a hanger and lay on the bed. Astonishment! Every dress but one. She hung it in the closet and shut the door. "That's what you will wear this week" was all she said. Then she bundled up my other dresses and left me speechless—as I had never been before that day—standing in the middle of my room.

The mortification, the consternation, the humiliation of having to wear the same dress to school every day for a week! But my little-girl pride was not the point of Mother's succinct lesson. Nor was her goal to instill in me a fetish for neatness. (It's a good thing!) Instead, her seven simple words marked the dawning of a new understanding in me about a myriad of greater issues: personal responsibility, self-discipline, care of one's (and even others') belongings, respect for other family members and the hard work they do for the sake of the family.

I must admit, I've never looked at my dresses the same way since.

Just Dessert

My favorite dessert as a kid was watermelon, and in the summertime Mama often gave us a big, juicy piece after supper. One night at bedtime, I begged, "Can I have another piece?... I haven't had a piece since supper."

"Yes, you have. Only a few minutes ago I cleaned up some seeds, juice, and a rind on the front steps."

"That wasn't me."

"Franklin! You know it was."

"It had to be somebody else...."

"Okay. Who?"

"I forget."

"Then remember."

"I can't."

"You know what I've told you about lying, Franklin. If you dare to tell a lie—"

"I'm not lying, Mama. I, well, I forget."

"Think hard."

"I can't."

"Let's get down on our knees. You ask the Lord to help you remember."...

"You pray first, Mama. Then I'll ask."

Mama started to pray, but it didn't sound as much like a prayer as it did a sermon about how the devil can get into your heart and take away your victory. Finally, she stopped. "Now you pray, Franklin."

"Dear Jesus," I began, "help a little boy remember…" I probably said more, but that's all I recall.

When I looked up, Mama stared at me. "Well?"

"He's not helping me very much."

"Oh yes, He is. He's already told you. You see, Franklin, He knows who ate the watermelon."

"Mama, God doesn't really know. He's just guessing."

"God never guesses. He knows everything. He sees everything."

"I'm beginning to remember now."

"What do you remember?"

"I was the one, Mama."

She put her arms around me. "If you had persisted in your lying, I would have had to take the belt to you," she said.

"I know, Mama, and I'm sorry."

Instead of spanking me, Mama brought me a small piece of watermelon, and it tasted a whole lot better than the piece I had sneaked out to the porch earlier that evening.

—FRANKLIN GRAHAM, *Rebel with a Cause*

A Mother-Teacher's Prayer

Heavenly Father,

You know what it's like to want to have children who obey You. You discipline us and give us guidelines for our own good and because of Your great love for us (Heb. 12:6).

May I share this motivation of Yours when I ask my children to obey. Lord, let my kids see that I obey You because I love You.

Your Word says not only is it right for children to obey their parents (Eph. 6:1) but also that it will go better with them all their lives if they do (Eph. 6:3). And, yes, it will go better for me, too. But I also pray that my kids will *want* to obey—not only for me, or to avoid trouble, but because it pleases You (Col. 3:20).

Make me a good example of obedience, Lord. Show me if I am doing anything to discourage or dishearten my children (Eph. 6:4), such as being inconsistent, inattentive, harsh, or plain old crabby. After all, I know it is Your kindness that leads us to repentance, not Your threats of punishment (Rom. 2:4).

Amen.

—DAVID AND HEATHER KOPP, *Praying the Bible for Your Children*

Discipline your son, and he will give you peace;
he will bring delight to your soul.

—PROVERBS 29:17

As mothers, we are makers of the men and women who can confront the coming generations with love and righteousness.

—BRENDA HUNTER, *The Power of Mother Love*

FIVE

Hands That Play

A mother's youthful ventures

We played, we sang, we danced wildly. And we
wandered quietly by the sea. I will always
remember these days in summer—
they are in my very being.

—HELEN THOMSON

GAVIN'S STORY

Two cups of coffee and two coconut supremes for $2.95. I counted the change, imagining that inflation could account for the discrepancy between today's transaction and similar ones in my memory. The total for the same items used to be right around $1.50. But that was years ago, and I didn't really care. Life was speeding by, and worrying about things like how much a few donuts cost would prevent me from catching up with it.

I probably didn't need to be invigorated any more than I already was, but stepping out of the warm donut shop into the cool morning air of the mountain town where I had grown up had that effect. For months my family and I had anticipated this summer visit to see my parents and get away from the bustle of Seattle. Hallelujah and we were finally here! If I hurried I would make it back to my parents' house before anyone but Mom, the earliest riser in the Appalachians, was awake. Sometimes I thought she had more energy than I did. But I found myself slowing down for a moment when I caught sight of the park across the street.

In the middle of the park, a gazebo on a peninsula stretched out over a glassy pond. I had skipped a lot of stones in that pond. Dad and I'd had a lot of conversations about girls (and more spiritual things, of course) under the massive pine next to the water. At the other end of the park were a few dilapidated tennis courts, which I couldn't believe were still there. Mom and I had played endless sets of tennis on those courts. I had pointed them out to her yesterday when we took the kids down to play at the jungle gym.

"We should've brought our racquets, Mom!" I teased her. "Maybe tomorrow."

"I'm too old for that now," she laughed, thinking (I guessed) of the arthritis that pained her knees. "But I could use the exercise!"

I could use the exercise. That's what she used to tell me on our way into the donut shop on our almost-daily summer tennis dates. There wasn't much for early risers to do in our small town, and I was too antsy an adolescent to park it and wait for my buddies to wake up. So, on most summer mornings, she and I would slip out of the house before my dad and brother were even awake, and we'd head for the courts.

We always stopped at the shop first. Two cups of coffee and two coconut supremes. The coffees were hers, the donuts mine. "Can't do anything before I have my coffee," she always said. I wiggled and squirmed and waited. In my opinion she never could drink that coffee fast enough.

Mom didn't like to play tennis much. Boggle was her game, and sometimes I could hear her up late at night rattling the letter cubes in their box, challenging herself and her dictionary to a match. *That* was not a game any of us were willing to sit and play with her. One word, six letters: b-o-r-i-n-g.

She might have said the same about tennis. Instead, she firmly instructed me over each second steaming cup of coffee that I was to run her around the court and make sure she got a workout. I was happy to comply.

Yesterday at the park, helping my youngest on the monkey bars, I realized for the first time why Mom had played hundreds of matches of a game she didn't like and never won. (She wouldn't ever tell me if she had *let* me win, but knowing her lack of athletic prowess I'd have to say I couldn't help but have the upper hand.) She knew that on one fast-approaching summer morning I would wake up and have a more important activity to attend to: fishing with friends, taking a job, waking up to a family of my own.... She knew those were my breaking-away years, and she was glad for those moments she had with me before the break became pronounced. Suddenly, there in the park with my family, I felt blessed.

Just as suddenly I realized the time.

It was slipping by. Adolescent boys don't have any notion of that concept. As a husband and father, now I do. These days it's my turn to consider the moments I have with Mom before she is the one gone forever.

I parked my car in front of my parents' old house and grabbed the bag of donuts off my front seat. Balancing one cup of coffee on top of the other, I began to creep up the creaky steps to their front door.

"Good morning." Her soft voice came from the corner of the front porch, as I had anticipated it would.

"Hello there," I said back.

"It's been awhile since you've been up this early," she observed.

I cocked my head to one side and held up the bag. "Had to run an errand."

She raised one eyebrow and smiled. "There wouldn't be two coconut supremes in that bag, would there?"

"And two cups of coffee to go with it." I handed her one and set the other on the rail.

"Too bad I can't move around a tennis court anymore," she said wistfully.

"But your mind's still quick." I said, sitting down next to her and resting my hand on her bony knee. "How about a game of Boggle?"

Forever Forts

"Oh, Mommy, come inside and see!" [Kevin and Laura] begged. Something inside Annie began to soften, and she got down on her hands and knees and crawled through a blanket-tunnel to a cozy little spot beside the coffee table. There she snuggled down beside her children, and suddenly the memories of her own childhood blanket forts began to overshadow the tug of her to-do list.... She remembered her own need to play as a child, and, with a pang, she recognized how she sometimes squelched this need in her children. Not today. Today she would embrace it.

"Okay, my children," she told them, nose-to-nose in the darkness. "Let's pretend that this fort is really a ship, and the rooms are the cabins!" Kevin and Laura opened their eyes wide with joy at their mother's spontaneous playfulness. "And we're here in the ship's library," she said, "so we need some books…" With that, Annie lifted the blanket, slithered out, and gathered an armload of library books and a flashlight. She returned and scrunched back into a spot between the two children, who laughed because her hair was sticking to the blanket-roof in static electric spikes. "Okay, let's read for a while, and then we'll have a picnic lunch in here," she announced. "Maybe, just maybe, we'll live in here *forever!*"

—ELISA MORGAN, *What Every Child Needs*

The Antidote

Leave it to a child to think being sick isn't such a bad thing. There was a time when I half looked forward to being relegated to the old sofa in our cheerful sunroom, even though we didn't own a VCR and Pong was the only video game in existence.

I didn't even mind when my younger sister would inevitably fall ill too. I didn't mind sharing the sofa or Grandma's afghans or the cat, who loved having a stationary lap (or two). I didn't mind at all, except when it came to the puzzles.

Whenever the bug would bite, Mom would take us first to the doctor, then to the store to pick out a puzzle. At home she would send us to put on our jammies, give us our pink medicine, and set up the portable chess table next to the sofa. Out came the box, up went the lid for reference, and there the three of us would sit until the puzzle was done or we had recovered.

Either one could take days. Usually three, with Mom's caring and playful presence.

Mom taught us the fun science of puzzle assembly. Turn every piece face-up. Assemble the border first. Group pieces according to color. Work from edge to center. Then she patiently stuck with us to the end, the hours passing, I suspect, more quickly for us than for her. My sister and I competed for the edge pieces, each determined to get the bulk of it done. But our bickering was destined to be brief. With her easy persuasion, Mom could somehow make another section as important as the border. And so my sister and I would once again find ourselves not minding that we were in each other's company.

It didn't take too many illnesses for us to graduate to increasingly complicated puzzles. The last I remember working on—a five-thousand-piece bouquet of wildflowers—we never did complete. Then I was older and came to prefer a good story to Mom's puzzles.

Leave it to a child to not know what she's missing. I didn't figure it out until I was too old and too far from home to ask Mom to work on a puzzle with me while I recovered. How many people get the chance to be sick without giving up playtime? Pretty much, I think, only kids whose moms know the secret.

—ERIN M. HEALY

When Mother Reads Aloud

When Mother reads aloud, the past
    Seems real as every day;
I hear the tramp of armies vast,
I see the spears and lances cast,
    I join the thrilling fray.
Brave knights and ladies fair and proud
I meet when Mother reads aloud.

When Mother reads aloud, far lands
    Seem very near and true;
I cross the deserts' gleaming sands,
Or hunt the jungle's prowling bands,
    Or sail the ocean blue.
Far heights, whose peaks the cold mists shroud,
I scale, when Mother reads aloud.

When Mother reads aloud, I long
    For noble deeds to do—
To help the right, redress the wrong;
It seems so easy to be strong,
    So simple to be true.
Oh, thick and fast the visions crowd
My eyes, when Mother reads aloud.

—ANONYMOUS

The Baby's Dance

Dance, little baby, dance up high,
Never mind baby, mother is by;
Crow and caper, caper and crow,
There little baby, there you go:
Up to the ceiling, down to the ground,
Backwards and forwards, round and round.
Then dance, little baby, and mother shall sing,
With the merry gay coral, ding, ding, a-ding, ding.

—ANN TAYLOR

When laughter is thin around our house, it's a sign that we're pushing too hard and need to lighten up. Our Lord came to give us joy, not stress.

Some of our best family memories are the spontaneous moments. One day just before the school bus came by to bring the kids home, our dog, Chester (the ugliest dog you ever saw), was at my feet while I was folding laundry. Chester always went out to meet the kids. I had a pair of Andy's Superman Underoos in my hand and thought, *Why not?* So I put them on Chester and sent him out to meet the kids.

The gales of laughter from the boys at the sight of Chester were worth it.

—NANCIE CARMICHAEL, *Lord, Bless My Child*

SIX

Hands That Teach

A mother's wise instruction

I learned more about Christianity from my mother
than from all the theologians of England.

—JOHN WESLEY

TERRI'S STORY

I met God in Arnie's diner across the street from my high school. Actually I'd met Him years back at summer camp, after hearin' Catherine Weaver's bring-'em-to-tears testimony and gettin' up front for the altar call. But I didn't *really* meet Him until Mama and I started meetin' for lunch at Arnie's.

Somethin' 'bout high school done opened my mind to the black and white and gray issues of the world and how faith fits in. Even back then in them calm days of the '50s I took God and my parents to task over plenty. I'd been askin' lots of questions in hopes of gettin' answers that would bring solid sense to Christianity, answers that would make me more comfortable with God. I s'pose I was lookin' for that false confidence that comes with feelin' "right." But I didn't know at the time 'bout nothin' false. All I knew was I didn't like those gray areas.

Mama picked up on this right away and wasn't content to leave my guidance wholly in the hands of Miss Becker, the nicest and smartest Sunday-school teacher you ever did meet. Nor did she consider the occasional youth rally enough to get me through. So she came to my room one evenin' before bed.

"I was wonderin'," she began, "if you'd be interested in studyin' the book of Romans together." The idea caught hold o' me. Durin' summer recess I'd picked up a decent amount of scintillatin' conversation from the ladies' Bible study Mama was a part of, which met every week at our house. But family devotions weren't the buzz then that they are today, and Mama and I had never done a study together.

We decided we'd read a chapter a week, and then we'd meet at Arnie's every Thursday durin' the school lunch hour to talk about it. Each of us would keep a journal for writin' down thoughts and questions. She wanted me to do some hard work, some wrestlin' with the meanin' of things, before we got together. That suited me just fine.

I got along well, albeit in fits and starts of understandin', sittin' in the red booth at the back of Arnie's to escape what noise we could. Mama was full of wisdom, which I figured she'd picked up from payin' such good attention to Reverend Wilde, then studyin' on her own. I figured I'd better start payin' more attention to Reverend Wilde myself.

When we came to chapter nine, though, I got stuck. "As it is written, Jacob have I loved, but Esau have I hated," I read in King James's poetic way of puttin' things. "What shall we say then? Is there unrighteousness with God? God forbid. For he saith to Moses, I will have mercy on whom I will have mercy, and I will have compassion on whom I will have compassion."

The passage ate at me the whole week, but I managed to let it simmer 'til Thursday. I sat down hard in our booth and set my ponytail floppin'. "How is that, Mama? How can God pick and choose who gets His mercy and then say it isn't unjust?" I felt a tad riled, but I was confident Mama would put my mind at ease.

She didn't. She talked some 'bout a similar verse in Exodus 33 where the Lord says, "I will…be gracious to whom I will be gracious, and will shew mercy on whom I will shew mercy." Then we talked 'bout Pharaoh and how God had hardened His heart against the Israelites. But that didn't come close to satisfyin' me. I wanted to know *why.*

Mama could've launched into a discussion 'bout God's foreknowledge, 'bout His sovereignty. She could've talked 'bout predestination or even what John Wesley had referred to as God's "terms" of justice. Instead she simply said, "I don't know, Terri. I don't understand it all either, but I believe God is just."

I returned to school feelin' frustrated and dissatisfied. And maybe a tad relieved. Mama had given me permission not to know. I'd wrestled and, try as I might, couldn't come up with any answer that put my mind at ease. Even so, I walked away with permission to not have the answers and still say, "But I believe."

I didn't see what Mama was tryin' to show me for a long time after, maybe even years after. But she'd seen my need to believe what I believed on some kind of head-smart level. She saw I was hungry for reason and watched me fight battles that could take reason down in the first round. She knew if I fought that battle for too long I would lose.

In those weeks when we met to talk 'bout Romans, she showed me how to give an answer for what I believed. But she also showed me how to cling to faith where it sure seemed reason left off.

I am still a "show me" learner. I still, on occasion, can be found beatin' my head against the metaphorical wall when, as a good friend of mine is fond of sayin', there's an open door two steps to the right! But, thanks to Mama, in spite of this ol' tendency of mine, I can still say, "I don't know the answer to that, but I believe!"

Marmee's Lessons

"Once upon a time, there were four girls, who had enough to eat and drink and wear, a good many comforts and pleasures, kind friends and parents, who loved them dearly, and yet they were not contented." (Here the listeners stole shy looks at one another, and began to sew diligently.) "These girls were anxious to be good, and made many excellent resolutions; but they did not keep them very well, and were constantly saying, 'If we only had this,' or 'If we could only do that,' quite forgetting how much they already had, and how many pleasant things they actually could do. So they asked an old woman what spell they could use to make them happy, and she said, 'When you feel discontented, think over your blessings, and be grateful.'" (Here Jo looked up quickly, as if about to speak, but changed her mind, seeing that the story was not done yet.)

"Being sensible girls, they decided to try her advice, and soon were surprised to see how well off they were. One discovered that money couldn't keep shame and sorrow out of rich people's houses; another that, though she was poor, she was a great deal happier, with her youth, health, and good spirits, than a certain fretful, feeble old lady, who couldn't enjoy her comforts; a third that, disagreeable as it was to help get dinner, it was harder still to have to go begging for it; and the fourth, that even carnelian rings were not so valuable as good behavior. So they agreed to stop complaining, to enjoy the blessings already possessed, and try to deserve them, lest they should be taken away entirely, instead of increased; and I believe they were never disappointed, or sorry that they took the old woman's advice."

"Now, Marmee, that is very cunning of you to turn our own stories against us, and give us a sermon instead of a romance!" cried Meg.

"I like that kind of sermon. It's the sort father used to tell us," said Beth thoughtfully, putting the needles straight on Jo's cushion.

"I don't complain near as much as the others do, and I shall be more careful than ever now, for I've had warning from Susie's downfall," said Amy morally.

"We needed that lesson, and we won't forget it. If we do, you just say to us, as Old Chloe did in 'Uncle Tom,' 'Tink ob yer marcies, chillen! Tink ob yer marcies!'" added Jo, who could not, for the life of her, help getting a morsel of fun out of the little sermon, though she took it to heart as much as any of them.

—LOUISA MAY ALCOTT, *Little Women*

I am eternally grateful to my mother for many things, but one of the most enduring blessings she brought into my life was to teach me the Catechism at the age of ten that "God is a Spirit, infinite, eternal, and unchangeable in his being, wisdom, power, holiness, justice, goodness, and truth." That definition of God has been with me all my life, and when a man knows in his heart that God is an infinite, eternal, and unchangeable Spirit, it helps to overcome the temptation to limit Him.

—BILLY GRAHAM, *Peace with God*

I put the relation of a fine teacher to a student just below the relation of a mother to a son, and I don't think I could say more than this.

—THOMAS WOLFE

Do not forsake your mother's teaching.

—PROVERBS 1:8

SEVEN

Hands That Protect

A mother's passionate defenses

God could not be everywhere and therefore
He made mothers.

—JEWISH PROVERB

SHEILA'S STORY

Snap! My teacher dropped—no, *threw*—the paper on my desk. My heart stopped and I forgot the punch line of a joke I was telling my friend Jackie. A big red F blazed across the top of my paper for the entire class to see. I could have died. Mrs. Jones had written a minuscule note next to it: "Sounds copied to me."

Copied? I couldn't believe it. I felt sick. Writing was what I did best. It was what I loved most. I always got terrific grades on my papers. *Copied?* As in *plagiarized?* No way. Where? What did she mean? I was too scared to ask her.

It was my last class of the day. I rushed home, slammed the door, and headed for my room. Mom was making dinner. "Hi, love!" she shouted after me. I guess my silence concerned her. She followed me to my room and stood in the doorway. "What's wrong?"

At first I was just angry. "Mrs. Jones says I copied my paper!" I threw it down on the bed. "She flunked me! How could she do that? She's so unfair!" Then the idea of it all settled in and I just started crying. Mom picked up the paper and read it.

"Did you ask her about it?"

"I couldn't," I sniffed.

She paused for a minute. "Did you copy it?" she asked softly.

"I don't even know what she's *talking about!*" I insisted.

I could feel her defenses rising for my sake. "Okay. Just a minute."

She left the room and I threw myself on the bed, waiting for her to come back. I heard her voice coming from the kitchen. "I'll be down in a few minutes. Thank you."

Oh, no. I bolted out of my room. "Oh, Mom—no!"

"We need to talk to her, Sheila. It's important." I would die of embarrassment. I would just *die.*

Twenty minutes later we were in Mrs. Jones's classroom. I fixed my eyes on the corner of her chic glasses, my embarrassment having given way to the hope that Mom would bring my teacher to her knees.

It was not to be. Apparently Mom had settled herself during the drive over. She was definitely speaking more respectfully than I had fantasized she would.

"I was hoping you could explain what this means," she said, referring to Mrs. Jones's note. "Sheila insists she didn't copy anything, so naturally I'm concerned."

Mrs. Jones's response was careful. "The level of writing here is far above what one would expect from someone her age. It's hard to believe she could come up with this on her own."

"She does write well," Mom said. *Darn right I do. Set her straight, Mom.* "This is her first paper for you, isn't it? Have you talked to any of her other teachers?" Mrs. Jones admitted she hadn't, but then pointed out my opening paragraph.

"This sounds remarkably like a dictionary definition," she said. My mother looked at me.

"How did you come up with this, love?"

Duh. It was a classic dictionary-definition opener, of course. But *I hadn't copied it.* I'd carefully changed the words so that they were my own. That was the way to do it, right?

I rolled my eyes as Mrs. Jones and Mom launched into a discussion about proper attribution. *Gimme a break. I learned all about that last year.* It wasn't necessary to attribute the dictionary, for goodness' sake, especially if the words were my own. That book is just...so...*public.*

Our fifteen-minute meeting that afternoon proved to be enlightening.

Mom and Mrs. Jones left the meeting relieved not to have had a more hair-raising confrontation. I left with an assignment to rewrite the first three paragraphs of my paper and a chance for a better grade.

On the way out Mom rested her hand on my shoulder. "That wasn't so bad," she said to the sky.

"Uh huh," I whispered, trying to figure out what had just happened. I had expected her to protect my reputation with my favorite teachers. She was supposed to defend my sacred position as her only daughter. Things hadn't gone as well as I had expected.

In fact, even though I was clueless then, they had gone much better. Ultimately, Mom had protected something much more important than the things I held dear.

She had protected my integrity.

Pursued

But stronger than all was maternal love, wrought into a paroxysm of frenzy by the near approach of a fearful danger. Her boy was old enough to have walked by her side, and in an indifferent case she would only have led him by the hand; but now the bare thought of putting him out of her arms made her shudder, and she strained him to her bosom with a convulsive grasp as she went rapidly forward. The frosty ground creaked beneath her feet, and she trembled at the sound; every quaking leaf and fluttering shadow sent the blood backward to her heart, and quickened her footsteps. She wondered within herself at the strength that seemed to be come upon her, for she felt the weight of her boy as if it had been a feather, and every flutter of fear seemed to increase the supernatural strength that bore her on, while from her pale lips burst forth, in frequent ejaculations, the prayer to a Friend above—"Lord, help! Lord, save me!"

If it were *your* Harry, mother, or your Willie, that were going to be torn from you by a brutal trader, to-morrow morning—if you had seen the man, and heard that the papers were signed and delivered, and you had only from twelve o'clock till morning to make good your escape, how fast could *you* walk? How many miles could you make in those few brief hours, with the darling at your bosom—the little sleepy head on your shoulder—the small, soft arms trustingly holding on to your neck?

For the child slept; at first the novelty and alarm kept him waking; but his mother so hurriedly repressed every breath or sound, and so assured him that if he were only still, she would certainly save him, that he clung quietly round her neck, only asking, as he found him-self sinking to sleep—

"Mother, I don't need to keep awake, do I?"

"No, my darling; sleep if you want to."

"But mother, if I do get asleep, you won't let him get me."

"No! so may God help me!" said his mother, with a paler cheek and a brighter light in her large dark eyes.

"You're sure, ain't you, mother?"

"Yes, *sure!*" said the mother, in a voice that startled herself, for it seemed to her to come from a spirit within, that was no part of her; and the boy dropped his little weary head on her shoulder, and was soon asleep. How the touch of those warm arms, the gentle breath-ings that came in her neck, seemed to add fire and spirit to her movements. It seemed to her as if strength poured into her in electric streams, from every gentle touch and movement of her sleeping, con-fiding child. Sublime is the dominion of the mind over the body, that for a time can make flesh and nerve impregnable, and string the sinews, like steel, so that the weak become so mighty!

—HARRIET BEECHER STOWE, *Uncle Tom's Cabin*

Tiger Moms

A reporter interviewing Daphne Gray, whose deaf daughter Heather Whitestone became Miss America 1994, describes her quality of hyperawareness: "A faraway look comes to her eyes when she speaks about what Heather can do, as if she hears something no one else can. As if having a deaf daughter means she hears extra." We mothers know that Daphne Gray *does* "hear extra." As do we. We hear, see, and feel things others don't even notice. Our experience—with its pain, vigilance, and hard work—has heightened our senses when it comes to our child. It is as if we have developed extra nerve endings. We are tiger mothers—ever watchful, ever ready—tireless to protect, provide, defend.

Sometimes we sense that others are wary of us. They feel—and fear—the great power within us, the fire burning in our eyes. We are tuned into something extra, something they don't hear.

—BARBARA GILL, *Changed by a Child:*
Companion Notes for Parents of a Child with a Disability

When she cried her deep soulful cry, I was filled not merely with panic but with passion. I loved her even more for not being beautiful. But was she comfortable? Were those sunbeams perhaps a little too strong? Did they cause her a moment's inconvenience? I would smash the sun to smithereens if they did. It would be the work of a moment: nothing easier. I would weep tears of anguish the while. There seemed to be lots of anguish about. I only had to imagine her suffering anything at the hands of anybody and I sprouted claws and fangs. I would tear her assailants limb from limb. Motherhood seemed to have turned me, overnight, into a sabre-toothed tiger.

—SUE LIMB, *Love Forty*

EIGHT

Hands That Serve

A mother's remarkable selflessness

A mother is completely fatigued. She has been telling
her friends for weeks that there is nothing left of her,
and then a child falls ill and needs her.
Week after week, by night and day, she stands by
and never thinks of being tired.

—HARRY EMERSON FOSDICK

A woman who is a true servant reaches out to others with movements so completely integrated into her way of life that it is often difficult to isolate a single gesture and say, "Herein lies a story." As best-selling author Ingrid Trobisch once said, "Women like to make sacrifices in one big piece, to give God something grand, but we can't. Our lives are a mosaic of little things, like putting a rose in a vase on the table."

My mother was the kind of woman who placed roses in other people's lives. In fact, she distributed her flowers so freely that many who knew her soon found themselves lying in a veritable bed of scented velvet petals. It was her way.

Distracted by the demands of a career, a ministry, a husband, and three teenagers, I did not fully realize the extent of my widowed mother's rose giving until she came to live with us. With cancer rapidly spreading throughout her body, her bright life was clearly waning. I wanted to have her close by, to celebrate her remaining days, to care for her more completely.

I suspect, however, that she did more for us than we did for her. On her good days I would catch her pressing my husband's shirts, applauding my daughter's fledgling attempts to learn the violin, or telling my son stories of Dad's football years. She filled a long-forgotten bird feeder outside the kitchen window and lured them back to visit. She cut flowers for the dining room table—how long had it been since I'd last done that?—and helped my youngest with his English assignments. While Mother was with us, our home was brighter than it had been in months.

Then she was gone, and it seemed for a moment that the brightness had gone too. But a woman like Mother can't take that kind of light with her, as became evident after the funeral.

Mrs. Knighten brought over a relish tray for the gathering after Mother's memorial. "She was a most thoughtful woman," Mrs. Knighten told me. "After my Jack passed on, she came over every day to visit and take care of my cats. Cats! Who but your mother would have thought of that? I had completely forgotten them."

Young Katie Arnold held my hand with tears in her eyes. Mother had taken Katie to church for years after her parents had divorced. "There were things I could tell your mom that I could never explain to anyone else. She understood me better than anyone ever has."

"I'll miss her," Pastor Davidson told me quietly. He gave me a handmade card signed by the kids she'd taught at Vacation Bible School. "It will be hard to find someone who can run our clothing drive as well as she could."

"She made the best chicken-noodle soup I have ever tasted! Could drive a cold away in a matter of minutes…"

"…still have the rag dolls she made for our girls the year we couldn't afford Christmas presents…"

"...that time she paid our utility bills until Ted could get a job again..."

"...picked up Jamie from school a dozen times when I'd get stuck in meetings..."

"...and she just held me and held me when I couldn't stop crying..."

The conversation whirled around me, and I smiled, knowing that even in her death she would inspire each of us who loved her to serve one another with the love of Christ, even as she had served us. We talked and remembered late into the night.

The next day I visited our florist and cleaned them out of their roses. "I'll take everything you have in stock," I told the startled girl at the register. "Yes, as many as you can spare." I drove to the cemetery and carried them all to my mother's grave, where the overturned earth and dozens of flower arrangements were still fresh.

"Thank you, Mother," I said aloud, laying one pink rose on top of the marker. After a few moments I took a walk around the perfectly manicured grounds, leaving a single rose on every grave that didn't boast a flower.

Roses in the name of the rose giver. Roses for those who had none. It's what she would have done.

The Rich Depression

I've never forgotten one brown velvet dress Mother made for me out of someone's hand-me-down. The velvet was worn in places, and the chocolate brown was wrong for a young girl. I suffered in silence every time I wore it. And my sister was mortified, she tells me, by never having a proper girl's snowsuit of her own, but having to wear an old pair of her brother's pants in wintertime....

Though we did without many things, Mother always provided us with a feeling of well-being. Chiefly, I think, because of the ways she contrived to give to others. Out of our meager pantry she would send a sick neighbor a supper tray of something delicious she had prepared—velvety-smooth boiled custard; feather-light homemade rolls—served up on our best china and always with a dainty bouquet from our garden....

Only unconsciously were we aware of it, but Mother was providing us constantly with an object lesson in giving. The message: No matter how little you have, you can always give some of it away. And when you do that, you can't feel sorry for yourself.

But there was even more to it. For Mother, giving was an act of faith, and the spiritual principle of giving out of scarcity came as easily to her as if she had invented it. Whenever we saw an old-fashioned pump in a farmyard, we knew what she would tell us: "If you drink the cup of water that's waiting there, you can slake your own thirst. But if you pour it into the pump and work the handle, you'll start enough water flowing to satisfy all our thirsts."

She likened the principle of priming the pump to God's law of abundance: We give, and He opens the windows of heaven and gives to us. It is a law of life, she explained to us children, and as certain to work as that the sun will rise tomorrow.

—CATHERINE MARSHALL

When driving in the family carriage from Blairbeth to Glasgow, Mother would frequently see a pale face pressed against the window high up in one of the tenements. One day she had the coachman stop the carriage and, alighting, made her way through the "close" and up the dark winding stairway to the chamber where she had seen the face at the window. There she found a frail, crippled girl. After that visit Mother started a Friday-night Bible class for mill girls…. Yes, Mother, thou hast reaped well indeed…. Not empty-handed didst thou go to the King's Gate.

—CLARENCE MACARTHEY, *The Making of a Minister*

She makes coffee in the mornings, gets her children off to school, and tries to make ends meet at the market. She is very bright, her snapping eyes tell me. Yet she serves. She manages here in this restaurant. She is capable of more.

That is something women everywhere share in common. Perhaps that is why they can make do, be happy wherever they are; they're used to making contentment out of whatever comes—always making something from nothing, stretching the stew, remaking the worn-out clothes or opportunity into something "new" and presentable, smiling and caressing in spite of their own inclinations to tears and fatigue—mothering the world.

—GLORIA GAITHER, *We Have This Moment*

NINE

Hands That Receive

A mother's unconditional acceptance

Children, look in those eyes, listen to that dear voice,
notice the feeling of even a single touch that is
bestowed upon you by that gentle hand. Make much
of it while yet you have the most precious of all good
gifts, a loving mother. In after life you may have
friends, fond, dear friends, but never will you have
again the inexpressible love and gentleness lavished
upon you, which none but a mother bestows.

—THOMAS BABINGTON MACAULAY

TODD'S STORY

I have a soft-focus memory of a particular moment involving my mother's eyes. Staring into mine, they overflow with love and ask for nothing except that I would take everything she has to give. The memory carries motion with it, a comforting back-and-forth rhythm. Maybe we were in a rocking chair.

I can't say whether the memory is truly mine or a composite assembled from what I saw as Mam looked at my younger brothers. Either way, I've chosen to own it, having no doubt that she has looked at each of us this way. Even if the images of infancy fade, the emotions and sensations don't.

Kevin arrived when I was eight, his birth surrounded by whispers and worried looks from Nana, who had come early to help. "There is something wrong with the baby," she told me in dramatic overtones with one hand on her bosom. "They'll be home tomorrow."

They came home. Pop looked exhausted, his posture begging me not to ask too many questions. Mam looked even more tired. Her eyes lit up when she saw me, and she gave me a longer hug than usual. "Todd, come meet your baby brother."

It was Down syndrome that made his eyes that shape, Pop told me later. Nana proclaimed that he would never be "normal" and told me I would have to take extra special care of him. I asked Mam about it.

"Kevin is different," she told me, "but no less deserving of our love. He is your brother and my son, sent to us by God. Nothing changes that."

That first year was a fragile one, with good days and bad. Once I caught Mam crying softly over Kevin's crib. I didn't know much about grief or disappointment then, but instinct told me to let her be. I was certain that Mam and Pop loved Kevin—they fed him, played with him, talked to him, bathed him. In time Mam began telling me stories of how she had done the same with me. She would smile, remembering. "I'm so glad to be your mommy," she would say to both of us. She smiled more often as the months went by.

One day when Kevin was almost two, Josephine Andler came knocking. Mrs. Andler was a kind lady from church who sometimes taught my Sunday-school class. She organized the mission fund and worked downtown with "troubled girls" (that's what Mam called them). Mrs. Andler gave me a grown-up handshake and asked me a few questions about school. Then she wanted to talk with Mam and Pop. They sent me to watch Kevin in the playroom.

But my ears burned, so I watched Kevin from just outside the playroom, leaning into the stairway to hear what I could of the downstairs conversation.

"...due soon...lots of tests...Down's likely...heard of you...won't keep it otherwise—"

"—of course we will," I heard my parents say in unison, interrupting her.

I could imagine Nana fainting.

Mitchell joined our family one month later, looking startlingly like

Kevin with his mop of black hair and his almond-shaped, chocolate-brown eyes. Mam and Pop brought him home from the hospital with light in their eyes and smiles on their faces. "Todd and Kevin, come meet your baby brother," Mam said.

A week afterward I awoke in the middle of the night and wandered into the hallway toward the bathroom. Soft sounds came from Mitchell's room, and I peeked in. He rested in the crook of her arm, and she didn't even see me. She watched him intently. His gaze matched hers. "God created your innermost being," she whispered to him. "He knit you together in your mother's womb. You are fearfully and wonderfully made, and I'm so glad to be your mommy."

It was then I remembered her eyes and the words they had spoken as she had rocked me. I was sure she had held me as she had often held Kevin and as she now held Mitchell. It was then I knew for sure, without a doubt, that, no matter what, she would always be glad to be our mommy.

Bear-Size Love

*What if I turned
into a polar bear,
and I was the
meanest bear you ever saw
and I had sharp, shiny teeth,*

and I chased you into your tent
and you cried?

Then I would be very surprised
and very scared.
But still,
inside the bear,
you would be you,
and I would love you.

—BARBARA M. JOOSSE, *Mama, Do You Love Me?*

Young children develop an understanding of who they are and how they are loved by absorbing descriptions of themselves from others. It is not an intellectual experience, but a feeling experience that comes from being in a relationship with another person, a mother especially.... Moms are the ones who live in the day-to-day world of their children, observing victory and defeat, acceptance and rejection, contentment and frustration. Moms are the ones who have a unique opportunity to influence their children by reflecting their preciousness. As mothers, we are our children's first mirror, reflecting back to them their worth. No wonder they stare deeply into each reflection we offer, taking it into their very souls!

—ELISA MORGAN, *What Every Child Needs*

Who is it that loves me—and will love me forever with an affection which no chance, no misery, no crime of mine can do away? It is you, my mother.

—THOMAS CARLYLE

TEN

Hands That Applaud

A mother's genuine encouragement

My mother was the making of me. She was so true, so
sure of me, and I felt that I had someone to live for;
someone I must not disappoint.

—THOMAS EDISON

KATIE'S STORY

I finally did it when I was twelve. The hours of practice, the scales and drills, the numerous lessons paid off, and after my fourth time competing—well, I'd never placed in a piano competition before. You'd be amazed. This time I placed third.

The event took place in a private home filled with rows of folding chairs. Those of us performing made tracks in the plush carpet leading to the grand piano, which stood in front of a sparkling picture window. I was next-to-last and bided my time by focusing on keeping my palms dry.

This was the part I hated most—the nervousness. No matter how hard I tried, no matter how many times I played in public, I had trouble getting over it. You know the feeling. The gurgling stomach, the thoughts run amok. It had caused me several heart-stopping gaffes. I hate to remember that time one judge wrote only "Not very well prepared" instead of the standard critique of several paragraphs. I kept waiting for the day when the anxiety would pass. Now, surrounded by the sounds of Beethoven and Mozart, I dreamed of what it would be like to play without shaking.

Eventually my turn came. I adjusted the bench and let my hands find their place on the keyboard. I closed my eyes. Never look at the keyboard. If you do, you'll lose your concentration.

I did the hardest piece first. Bach. Get it over with. Then the

Chopin. A flowing waltz with a couple of tricky spots. I finished it, startled. I hadn't made a single—but I wouldn't think about that yet. My hands stopped shaking just a little, and I began my favorite piece with more confidence: a bellowing Rachmaninoff that appealed to the melancholy in me.

Then it was over. I caught my mother in the corner of my eye as I gave my little bow. She was the only person fully aware of how difficult these performances were for me. She grinned. She applauded more enthusiastically than anyone else in the room. I hope you have someone like her in your life.

They announced the winners the following week, and my proud teacher called. Congratulations, she said, and keep the Rachmaninoff in good condition. Each of the pianists, including those from other regional competitions, would play at a winners' recital in two weeks.

At the recital I was less nervous than I had ever been. I sat apart from my mother with the other players. I was glad she would hear me in this setting.

I sat down and went through my routine: Adjust the bench. Find the keyboard. Close my eyes. Begin.

I played the first four bars. Then nothing. My mind went blank. I completely forgot what came afterward. The audience was quiet.

I paused. This had happened to me before. If I could just find my bearings, I knew I could make it through. I began again.

You can guess what happened next. Four bars, then nothing. Not even a memory of the melody. I tried three times, fumbling around— I genuinely thought I'd eventually hit the right note. But it had fallen off the keyboard, left the building, gone to Australia. I turned and found the eyes of my instructor, mouthed the words "I'm sorry," and slipped off the bench. A smattering of polite applause rippled through the room. Through tears of embarrassment I managed to find my mother's face. She still wore a smile as big as the one on the day of the competition, and she applauded as sincerely now as then.

"I'm so proud of you," she said afterward.

"Yeah, right," I mumbled. I was just angry.

"It took courage to keep trying." I was silent. Still mad. "Just because you forgot doesn't change the fact that you are gifted."

"I'm never going to play in public again," I announced. When you're twelve, you can be pretty definitive about life.

She was thoughtful. "I hope you change your mind. But even if you never play for another human soul, don't forget that this ability is God's gift to you. You play beautifully. I imagine He loves to hear you play as much as I do."

I did play in public again—when you're twelve, you can also be flexible—this time for our church worship team and then later for a local band that performed at street fairs and the like. Mom prompted me to write a few simple compositions of my own, which—well, I never wrote them down, but I have a recording somewhere. She even sent the family piano with me when I moved away from home.

So my mother's encouragement drove me forward to fame and fortune and fulfillment—I guess that's what I'm supposed to say, but you know it's not true, so I won't lie. I never did get over the shaking nervousness of playing in public, and eventually I gave up performing.

Even so, the words Mom spoke to me about giftedness go a long way in times when I feel I don't have anything to offer God or the world.

I remember her words when I make fumbling attempts to serve others through my gifts. I remember her confidence and manage to keep pressing on despite embarrassing errors. Her affirmation was persistent, continuous, and sometimes even relentless. And every once in a while I'll find myself sitting at that piano, just God and me, and I can believe He's smiling at me.

Against the Odds

Judy's mother, Anita Sutton, snapped photo after photo of Judy in her college graduation gown, both before the commencement ceremony and as Judy celebrated afterward.

Anita and her husband never stopped smiling. Finally they pulled their daughter into the kitchen, still grinning. "We have something we want you to know," her mother said. Judy, bewildered, looked at her mother's shining face.

"Judy, honey, when you were in junior high, your class took some standardized tests ordered by the school district. When the results came back, we were called to the counselor's office and told, 'You should know that, based on your daughter's test scores, she probably will never graduate from high school.'

"We decided not to tell you because we didn't want you to get it into your head that you couldn't graduate. Instead we decided to do everything in our power to help you do the best you could.... We told the counselor he must never show you the results. Then I got a little feisty and told him you *would* graduate—not only from high school but from college too."

As Judy listened, memories darted across her mind of all her parents had done to help her study during high school. She'd had a difficult time with some of her classes, but every afternoon her mother had helped her study, and her father had tutored her in math.

"We probably never would have told you at all if you hadn't decided to be a teacher," her mother said. "But we knew we had to tell you now so you wouldn't make that counselor's same mistake and tell parents their child couldn't do something. We want you to be optimistic about every child's potential and suggest positive, concrete ways parents can help. We're proud of you, honey. You proved those test givers wrong!"

Judy's eyes filled with tears as she hugged her parents and managed to whisper a hoarse "Thank you."

Today Judy is married to a chaplain with the California Youth Authority. In addition to her work as assistant pastor of care ministries at a large church, she is solidly pursuing an M.A. degree in pastoral care and counseling. She loves pointing out the strengths of those who feel as though they have no gifts and suggesting ways they can use their talents for ministry. And to think it all started with Judy's mother's refusal to let a school counselor's negative assessment hold her daughter back.

—SANDRA P. ALDRICH AND BOBBIE VALENTINE, *HeartPrints*

Dearest,

Accept this pen from your mother and for her sake use it freely & worthily that each day of this your fifteenth year may testify to some good word or thought or work.

I know there will be born into your spirit new hopes, new gifts, for God helps the loving, trusting heart that turns to Him. Lift up your soul to meet the highest, for that alone will satisfy your yearning, aspiring nature.

Your temperament is a peculiar one, & there are few who can really help you. Set about the formation of character & believe me you are capable of obtaining a noble one. Industry, patience, love, creates, endures, gives all things, for these are the attributes of the Almighty, & they make us mighty in all things. May eternal love sustain you, infinite wisdom guide you, & the peace which passeth understanding reward you, my daughter.

Mother

Nov. 29th, 1846

—ABIGAIL MAY ALCOTT,
in a letter to her daughter, Louisa May Alcott

Mama exhorted her children at every opportunity to "jump at de sun." We might not land on the sun, but at least we would get off the ground.

—ZORA NEALE HURSTON

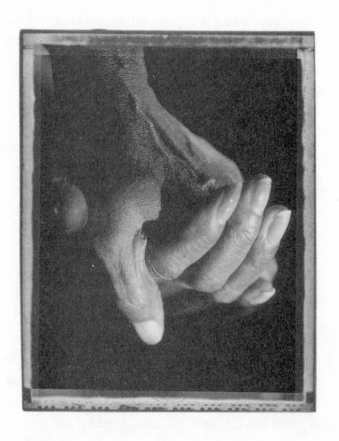

ELEVEN

Hands That Pray

A mother's deepest longings

For this child I prayed.

—1 SAMUEL 1:27 (KJV)

ELAINE'S STORY

I'm not sure when we started saying grace. It didn't mean much to me; I just figured it was something every Christian family did. But I was almost nine, that awkward age when the world bursts wide open and you start to notice things, when I realized Mom was the only one praying over our meals.

"Mommy, how come Daddy doesn't say grace?"

The thoughtful answer came after a pause. "He's not ready to yet, honey."

"Why not?"

And then my world really did burst wide open, and I spent the afternoon on my bed in quiet tears because I hadn't known before then that my daddy didn't know God. Sometimes it hurts when you start to notice things.

Mom sat next to me and stroked my head. My father is a good man, and he was then too, and Mom explained that sometimes it's hard for good people to believe they need God. Daddy didn't believe it himself quite yet.

"So what are we going to *do?*" I asked with all the melodrama a nine-year-old can muster.

"We'll pray for him," she said. And we did. She did, anyway. And it was a pretty fancy prayer, I thought, much better than I could ever do, and I wondered, *With prayers like those to listen to, why would God need mine?*

I started taking more notice of her mealtime prayers. I couldn't match her for style or content but figured it would only take time, so I listened out of both ears and watched her out of one eye. Sometimes her blessings would get long—she just couldn't help but tell God everything—and Daddy would gently squeeze her hand and she'd wrap things up with a smile. "Sometimes I get a little carried away, don't I?" I wasn't sure that was such a bad thing.

Each night I'd try an elaborate new prayer. Each morning I sneaked a peek at Daddy but couldn't tell if his eyes were open or closed. And he hadn't volunteered to take over the blessings yet. When would it happen?

I woke up early one morning and found Mom reading her Bible while our cat napped in the sun that fell across her lap.

"What are you doing?" I whispered. The scene required a whisper.

She motioned me over. "Praying," she said quietly.

"I don't think God is hearing my prayers," I said.

"Why not?" she asked. I think she knew.

"They're not as good as yours."

I squeezed into the chair next to her and upset the cat, and he protested but then resettled himself. "God is more interested in what you're praying about than whether your prayers sound like mine," Mom said.

"But you always know what to say, and I don't know the right words or how to keep talking for so long."

"Say what you're thinking," she urged me. "Your prayer doesn't have to be fancy or long. God is listening to you, even if it seems He isn't."

Maybe she was right. Even at age nine, I knew she usually was. So I quit trying to pray like Mom did and resorted to a single plea, which I couldn't say more simply or mean more passionately: "Dear Jesus, please help Daddy come to know you." That was all. Every night for a year.

Then one morning Daddy came in to wake me up, and he sat down on my bed in the dim light of the pulled window shade. "I wanted to tell you what I did last night," he said quietly. Mom had told him I'd want to know.

"Oh," I said quietly after he finished talking. I sat and stared at him and wondered, *What else could I say?* My perplexed father returned to his room and asked Mom to explain, but I don't think she knew any more than he did.

It took a few minutes for the realization that God had answered my prayers to set in, but when it did, I whooped and hollered my way down the hall and woke up my sister. I glowed more than Daddy did.

I've since learned a great deal more about prayer, more about the asking and the answering and the praising and the repenting. The mechanics of prayer—a topic in every pastor's repertoire, in every Christian bookstore—are easy to come by, but the spirit of it is harder to find. Today, as a woman with children of my own, I have a much better sense of what it means to pray passionately, as my mother always has, whether for her family or for complete strangers halfway around the world. I still have an inkling that my prayers are not quite as good as hers, although I know that's not the point. But she will always be a model.

She still wakes early to talk to God. He is present at every meal she serves, her long list of blessings still an opportunity to tell God what's on her heart. She is the first person who comes to mind when I need someone to pray with. I long for her prayers, which come from decades of knowing and loving God. And I'll call her, and we'll talk, and she'll say, "Let's pray," and we will. She'll do the bulk of the praying, and then she'll close with smiling words. "Sometimes I get a little carried away, don't I?"

Warrior Prayers

I watch my five-year-old lower himself into the steaming tub where Mr. Bubble ministers to the wounds my son has suffered in battle today.

His arms bear scratches from the apple tree he scaled, and both knees are streaked with bloody reminders of his encounter with the sidewalk while charging on his trusty Huffy.

Gently I towel down his bruised thighs, dotted with bites from relentless mosquitoes.

With vigor I rough up his sun-bleached hair and shoo him into his room where he dresses himself for bed.

A story, a prayer, a hug, and a kiss.

My brave warrior closes his eyes, and I stand back, marveling that this long, sturdy body, lying lumpy beneath the covers, once fit in my arms and nursed at my breast.

Many summer nights, just like this one, I rocked him. For hours I rocked and I sang and I prayed. Oh, how I prayed!

I close his door softly. My soldier needs his sleep.

Tomorrow great battles will be fought…in the sandbox, on his skateboard, with the neighborhood kids. He will return to me, bloodied and bruised, and there will be so little I can do. I have no power over scraped knees and stubbed toes.

But the real battle—the one not against flesh and blood but against principalities and powers of the air—has already begun in his young life.

And in that battle, I am the warrior.

I pray.

Oh, how I pray!

That God will have the ultimate victory.

—ROBIN JONES GUNN, *Mothering by Heart*

Daily

And all the angels everywhere…
Hear mother's love as it fills the air
Day and night I say this quiet prayer
"Lord, keep my child in your care."

—BONNIE KNOPF, *As I Kneel*

It pleased God to keep me a long time without a child, which was a great grief to me and cost me many prayers and tears before I obtained one, and after him gave me many more of whom I now take the care, that as I have brought you into the world, and with great pains, weakness, cares, and fears brought you to this, I now travail in birth again of you till Christ be formed in you.

—ANNE BRADSTREET, in a letter to her eight children

The God who made your children will hear your petitions. He has promised to do so. After all, He loves them more than you do.

—JAMES DOBSON, *Parenting Isn't for Cowards*

Hands That Release

A mother's greatest sacrifice

The maternal instinct…is a Gift-love…. But the
proper aim of giving is to put the recipient in a state
where he no longer needs our gift. We feed children in
order that they may soon be able to feed themselves;
we teach them in order that they may soon not need
our teaching. Thus a heavy task is laid upon this
Gift-love. It must work towards its own abdication.

—C. S. LEWIS

JASON'S STORY

After Ma dropped me off for college, she cried all the way home. That's what Francine, Ma's best friend, told me later. Ma held up just fine while she was there with me, stacking sheets in my cramped dorm closet and putting books on the makeshift shelf of pine boards and cinder blocks. "You need a reading light for your desk," she announced suddenly. Then she burst out the door and was back in twenty minutes with one from a nearby hardware store.

From her hulking purse she pulled a wrinkled grocery bag filled with every medicine a college student could ever need. She took inventory of my wardrobe to make sure I would be warm through the cold Chicago winter. She made a note to send me Pa's heavy down jacket "just in case." She wrote down her calling card number even though I already had it and tacked it to my bulletin board. She took Francine and me out to dinner, and then there was nothing left for her to do. She stood at my yawning door and gave me a tight hug. I was thinking that the orientation programs had begun ten minutes ago and, really, I shouldn't get there too late. Francine gave me a wink and a wave and quietly ducked out of the dorm to wait in the car.

When Ma released me, my thoughts shifted. She ran her soft hand through my spiky hair and said gently to my forehead, her thoughts far away, "May the Lord bless you, and keep you, and make His face to shine upon you, and give you peace."

Ma had spoken those words to me hundreds of times as I grew up. She'd started saying them sometime when I was in elementary school, when I didn't really get it. She said them all the way through my junior high school years, when I secretly liked the benediction but dreaded getting caught by my friends. Ma knew that, though, and was discreet. She'd stop me whenever I was running out the door during high school—I was always running out the door—and I would stand under her loving eyes thinking, with some guilt, "Yeah, yeah, Ma...Hurry up!"

But when she said those words that day in my new home-away-from-home, I heard them for the first time.

"May the Lord bless you, and keep you, and make His face to shine upon you, and give you peace."

She gave me a quick kiss and one last hug. "I can't wait to see you at Thanksgiving," she said. Then she flashed a stoic smile and disappeared into the stairwell. I closed my door and stood in the dark, grateful that my roommate had already gone to orientation. It was another ten minutes before I arrived there myself.

Today I'm looking over the rim of a steaming coffee cup, remembering that moment. I pretend to read the newspaper, but in reality I'm watching my wife adjust our five-year-old's backpack straps. The pack is bigger than he is, and how he can stand up under it I don't know. Low center of gravity, I guess. My wife picks imaginary lint off his shirt, feigning excitement. "You look *terrific*," she says. "Think of all the new friends you're going to make at school! Grab your coat and let's go."

I set the paper down and follow my son into his room, a five-year-old's monument to disaster. He picks through the rubble looking for his coat. "Ready for your big day, Jake?" I ask. He doesn't look so sure. I hesitate for just a second, then get down on my knees. "C'mere, Bud," I say. He momentarily abandons his search and reaches out to give me a hug, and I know I won't get to do this for much longer. His fine brown hair threatens to stick in my teeth, but I manage to whisper:

"May the Lord bless you, and keep you, and make His face to shine upon you, and give you peace."

Independence Day

On my first day in the first grade, I panicked and cried and raced back to the car where my mother was, ran top speed before she drove away from me.

"Mama! Take me home!"

I thought she would be so happy to see me and to discover my undiminished need of her presence, her love and her protection. I sat smiling in the front seat and heard the car's ignition even before she turned the key. She never turned the key.

Only now do I understand her own tears as she took my hand and walked me back into the school again.

"Mama, do you hate me?"

"No! Not at all. I love you—"

What she was saying was, "Go away from me—in order to *be*."

So here I am, all done with first grade and writing books like any independent adult, and it is done. My mother sorrowed in the separation; but I am, by miracle, her joy and her accomplishment. Both. It is an astonishing act of love.

—WALTER WANGERIN, JR., *Measuring the Days*

Empty Nest

When each of you shall in your nest
Among your young ones take your rest,
In chirping language, oft them tell,
You had a dam that loved you well,
That did what could be done for young,
And nursed you up till you were strong,
And 'fore she once would let you fly,
She showed you joy and misery;
Taught what was good, and what was ill,
What would save life, and what would kill.
Thus gone, amongst you I may live,
And dead, yet speak, and counsel give:
Farewell, my birds, farewell adieu,
I happy am, if well with you.

—ANNE BRADSTREET,
from *"In Reference to Her Children, 23 June, 1659"*

At last they came to the pinnacle of the highest mountain. Beyond it they saw a shining road and a golden gate flung wide. There stood the brilliant tree of life. The mother said, "I have reached the end of my journey. I have been faithful to my children and faithful to God. The end is better than the beginning, for my children can walk alone with the Shepherd."

—LINDA DILLOW, *A Mother's Journey*